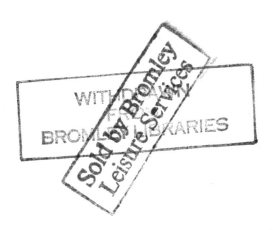

NEW & SELECTED POEMS

I.A.RICHARDS

New & Selected Poems

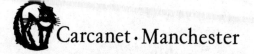

Carcanet · Manchester

ACKNOWLEDGEMENTS

Acknowledgements are due to the editors of *The American Scholar, Times Literary Supplement, PN Review, New Statesman* and *Spectator*, where some of the new poems first appeared.

First published in 1978 by
Carcanet New Press Limited
330 Corn Exchange
Manchester M4 3BG

The publisher acknowledges the financial assistance of the Arts Council of Great Britain.

Printed in Great Britain by
Billing and Sons Ltd.,
Guildford, London and Worcester.

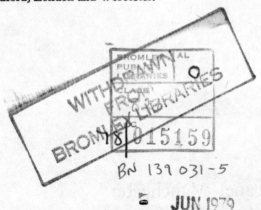

CONTENTS

6

FOREWORD

WITH THE Selected poems I am following Coleridge in thinking that the chronological order may be best, though I cannot be sure that the sequence is more than approximately correct. With the New poems, however, their bearings, one to another, may be brought out better by another order. 'Ars Poetica', though, is both the last New poem here presented and the latest to be written.

I. A. R.

from GOODBYE EARTH *(1958)*

AT THE MIRROR

Ah yes, the heart-ache friend
   Out there before you:
     The light-handed
       World-worn
     Nimble-witted
     Thrice-born
Comprehending, leisurable mind;
All yours and
   Eager to adore you.

Turn up the light!
O it is you there
You again
To whom each care:
   The dodging hope
The thin insight
   The narrowed scope
The famished wish
   The maiming shame
The bare despair,
   So freely came.

Who is the third
Stands by without a word?
Who watches this mistake?

How see the familiar I
Peer almost hourly through itself
Then sigh
Then steal and steel its own one eye:
In this world wake
In that world sleep
Each pervious to the other's ache.
—Who weaves this spell?—
How see all this and yet not see as well!

December—April 1953-4

LIGHTING FIRES IN SNOW

Tread out a marble hollow
    Then lay the twigs athwart,
        Teepee-wise or wigwam,
So that the air can follow
    The match-flame from the start:
        As we begin a poem
    And some may win a heart.

For twig to twig will beckon
    If lightly laid above
Better than you can reckon.
        Waste no time devising.
    No, no, it is not love,
        But the drying fume arising
    If the draft be free enough.

As the under cavern reddens
    Leave well alone!
Cold fuel only deadens.
        But pile across the smoke
    And give the dog a bone.
        For its life's sake, don't poke!
    The wise fire knows its own.

The wise poem knows its father
    And treats him not amiss;
        But Language is its mother
To burn where it would rather
    Choose that and by-pass this
        Only afraid of smother
    Though the thickening snow-flakes hiss.

THE SOLITARY DAFFODIL

From committee-doodled day
Beckon'd by the cocktail roar,
Feeling for what seemed a way,
I groped, as I had groped before.
A vivid Presence in the grass
Held me up. I could not pass.

A solitary Daffodil!
Its candid countenance was there
Speaking of the end of ill
With mild, confiding, tranquil air:
Its crisp, translucent whorls so pure
I grew as sure as it was sure.

Through golden depths *on on* it spoke,
A little Trumpet, grave and deep,
And nodded lightly as it woke
The world from transcendental sleep.
Alone had it been waiting there
A Herald and a Harbinger.

So, as a lost word found can say
The never-so-well-known-before,
It welcomed me into a Day
And almost opened me a Door
Through which I may still step to be
In recollected Company.

FORFEITS

Here is a thing;
And a very pretty thing;
What shall I do with
This very pretty thing?

What have I in my hand?
Staff of command?
Ho! Ho! Field Marshal, let,
Let call
This collieshangie off
Before worse harm.
Let beat retreat.
To dodge defeat,
Today,
The only way
Is only to Disarm!

Here is a thing;
And a very pretty thing;
What shall I do with
This very pretty thing?

What have I in my hand?
A baton to conduct
What I select?
Ha! Kappelmeister, set
Our wishes in array,
Duly in line,
And then let
Them
Intone
Their own
Fine
Requiem!

Here is a thing;
And a very pretty thing;
What shall I do with
This very pretty thing?

Still in my hand!
How lay
This ghost,
Or charm, or sign!
A pretty thing
To cling:
This role, this post
Unknown, unconned.
Lay down, lay down,
Old Clown,
Lay down
That Conjuror's wand!

North Conway 17 November 1957

BUT STILL DESIRE AND WILL . . .

Legs be still!
Far enough you've walked
Under, up and across
Hill over hill.

What! Are you twitching still?

Heart be still!
Times enough you have balked
Battened on mortal dross
Gobbled your fill.

What! Are you hungry still?

Tongue be still!
Long enough have you talked
Laying out gain and loss
Wish beside will . . .

Would you prophesy still?

Mind be still!

RAINBOW

Balanced up somehow on a ball
   That spins
      And spirals
         As it plummets,
   Newton walked to Stourbridge Fair
      And bought his prism
That was to fell the founding wall
   Undo the
      All
   Renew the
        Fall
         Bound through all limits
   And far and here declare
     The mere abysm.

Without——within! We were that idle void
   Its dust
      Its ashes
         Its endurances
   Its fled shrunk coils of stars
      Its wistlessness
Till we our Selves destroyed.
   The net
      We knit
   To sweep
      The deep
         Outwit the yet-perchances
   Took with it what else bars
     Existlessness.

O sole observer! Only unobserved!
   Neglected
      Left out
         Son of trouble!
   O knower glassier than the wave
     You float on,

Fish-serpent, winged and nerved,
   Invisible
      But still
   The source (which way
      you will)
         Of each least pressure building in the bubble:
   Is it not time to try your brave
      New coat on?

Open, entire, surrendered and serene
   'Seemeth'
      And maybe
         'That concordant one',
   Unlatched, a-swing to whatso'er
      Might lurk without.
But what's left out when naught's within?
   The sky
      Washed clean
   The dry
      Staff green,
         The circle won,
The pure light blossoms everywhere
   Out of the doubt.

THE STATUS OF THE MENTIONABLE

I.

The unmentionable is with, in, of me: me.
The mentionable turns object, over against;
Not me, not me: my shell.
And we who mention, we,
Are never what is mentioned.
What pure eye
Ever yet beheld the beholder?

My woven and compacted shell,
My global roof,
I tap and probe.
My diamond drill
Billions of light years off
Brings in its proof.
Uncrackable
And well
Defended still,
It is,
This shell.

How not behold the beholder?
My extant shell
That Eye projects;
Its diamond rays
Billions of lifetimes older
That shell reflects.
What's kept, it says,
By what is scrapped,
It says,
Is kept.

II.
Hill, cloud, field, wall . . .
All that we touch, see, think . . .
Unliven all: the stone, the dust
The Earth itself and men and Man
Turn thing
And must.

Will, doubt, desire, thought . . .
All in us:
Faith, Hope, Love . . .
Naught but THINGS itself away
And you, and I, as meant, obey:
Are noun'd
To naught.

Meanwhile,
Hill, cloud, field, wall . . .
As word with word
Unmeant, unheard, unseen,
Will, willy-nilly, mean.

TANTALUS

O tongue-tip hung the word sublime
    Would sum-up all All would have said
While temples tumbled on through time
    And tombs were buried with their dead.

Chance shakes none that; but—know no doubt—
    Design alone will not avail.
Though their each move be worked right out
    The servants of my servants fail;

And they I am. What we have been
    Stands here to limit what we tell
Unless, unless . . . that random scene
    Re-utter us and all be well.

LANDFALL

'The Other Shore, or Farther Bank, is the realm of ultimate truth and transcendental reality in contradistinction to This Shore—the bank on which we are standing, moving and talking, fettered by desire, subject to suffering.'—Heinrich Zimmer: *Myths and Symbols in Indian Art and Civilization.*

'Here or Nowhere is America.'—Goethe

Those Masters of that Farther Shore
Timeless at length
Forget all time
And all o'ercome before:
Lost is the Life and lost the Loss
And the journey across.

Benign, insuperable, Sublime,
They have the Strength
In Life to kill it
While up its dying boughs they climb.
Yet when they're there they know
It was none of it so.

No Life, no struggle to unwill it,
No length or Strength,
No voyage and no Shore,
No yonder
And no here,

No less, no more
No Law, no errors to fulfil it,
No Climb, no World, no World-forsaking
And no Awakening.
All Worth
Dissolved in Mirth—
All they knew, with all that knew, is gone,
The Scene, the Stage, such things might linger on.

THE THRONE

Not Eve herself is more
Than these Far-Shoremen are
The placard of a Dream
Set up this side the Stream
—Here, on this Hither Shore—
Man's hopes and aims to bar
And scenery to mar.

Nor is it less Desire
—The burning hand and eye—
Designs these Posters here
In outcries of despair:
'Put out, put out the Fire!'
Our Selves to twist awry
And Destiny deny.

The Tongue—itself a flame
And hotter when it's still—
Heats the insurgent Heart
—Silent on either part—
Until white-lit to claim
Through the usurping Will
Old shoes we cannot fill.

Not so the Lotus Throne
Or Who dream-wakes thereon
See now between the Two
—Look we both at and through
Bronze or lacquer or stone—
Within the hither and yon
Seeker become the Known.

RETORT

'Eternity is in love with the productions of Time.'
—Proverb of Hell

A poem's not on a page
        Or in a reader's eye;
    Nor in a poet's mind
Its freedom may engage.
        For I, a poem, I
    Myself alone can find
    Myself alone could bind.

I, though I take from you
        All, all I have to sing,
    Am all an empty Ought
Spinning itself its clew.
        Burning up what you bring
    To search out what you sought,
    I work on out from naught.

Eyeless, a source of seeing,
        Careless, a fount of care,
    An unrecorded vow
Is all my core of being.
        Yet, neither here nor there
    And with no then but now,
    Your life I disallow.

I sing, who nevertheless
        No accents have or breath.
    I neither live nor die.
But you whom I possess . . .
        You, you know life and death
    And throughly know; so I
    What void I fill thereby.

THE RUINS

The taste of time's beyond our wit
Like the lamb's bleat, the donkey's bray
A-sway on the edge of the eternal wall
Soon earthquake-juggled crazy; like the stray
Verse that if it could would say it.

The broken nose and the lost hand
May now enhance the statue's pose:
See for yourselves you may and take
Your own good will for deed—by those
Connivances our weakness won't withstand.

Nor scorn the syllables defective here
To take a sly advantage of their fault:
Blackleg a local strike or so, they will,
Or jerry-rig; since to the dear deaf ear
All words come cuckooing out of the same vault.

You do not trade too long upon a lack,
And words in poems have rights, say out their say,
Exact and render strict account,
Have little mercy on what's seen its day
Or could betray: all in the troth of the pack.

Sometimes a word is wiser much than men:
'Faithful' e.g., 'responsible' and 'true'.
And words it is, not poets, make up poems.
Our words, we say, but we are theirs too
For words made man and may unmake again.

To be at once explicit and elliptic
Both they and we play spillikins today
In homage to the log-jam and the landslide:
Lost nestless ants aclambering in the hay
Where some old, rusty, parting wire has flipt it.

So which way's which is now no more a query
And up or down's as free as heads or tails.
Without a centre or a pull to check it
The very sense of that dimension fails:
Rise! Fall! Sink—swim? All idle theory.

To take its place we have a wide selection
Of sweepings from the folklore merchants' floors
Pickings from anthropology's kitchen midden.
Come, cross yourselves at the museum doors
Before you add yourselves to the collection!

Did science answer only as to science
A faith could keep its converse for its own.
But 'WHAT AM I?' is the end of all enquiry
And what it turns on straight is turned to stone.
(A Gorgon of that grade's no mean appliance.)

Ah! deadliest aid to mental indigestion,
Solvent can settle all, beside yourself—
Nothing whatever left upon the tapis,
Were you not firmly kept upon the shelf:
What's made you ask yourself your final question?

In the museum now. And no one's here
Who isn't in for life—as an exhibit,
As a museum, no less, without the labels.
Museum specimens! Should the thought inhibit?
What has an instance left to hope or fear?

Round us in the clear and lighted spaces
The bones of statuary appear to stand
Stripped clean of the original blaze of colour
And dressed anew by Time's irreverent hand
To match the hid amazement on their faces:

'Never to be more honoured or regaled!
For all we were to have no mediation!
No solace but your impotent regard!
Poor token of your blinded adoration
Had you beheld before our beauty failed!

'The ecstasies our sanctuaries cherished
Were not as yours (for you have yours, no doubt
Beyond the compass of our divination)
What makes you go about so and about
To care so much for so much that has perished?'

Now their high structures all asprawl lie scattered,
Palace and temple, débris in the sun;
The faiths they sheltered every bit as weathered,
Disjointed just as much by excavation:
As if the record were the thing that mattered.

We excavators are in ruins too
Would need some rare successor to restore us
—Suppose he found our remnants worth his trouble—
'Judge not and ye shall not be judged.' It's true;
On each research research in turn is due.

Leave us well hid beneath our heaps of rubble.

Odysseus chose the lot that's out of view:
Happy the town or man sans history.
Maybe none's such and the least thing we do
Or leave undone within this mystery,
So burry is the seed, is sifted through.
So leads this parable—by the fall-line too:
'All's all rehearsal for the grand adieu.'

June 1955:
Delphi, Parnassus, Knossos, Epidaurus, Cyllene

MICROCOSMIC SONG

About the boundless yard may trudge
But victim, culprit, hangman, judge.

Victim rejoice! Your bitter end
Helps the primal hurt mend.

And culprit sing: 'Traitor's blow
Cuts through knots in Even So.'

Grave hangman smile: your gentle hands
Loose the noose none withstands.

But of the Judge, whom all must seek,
Little of him do wise men speak.

Victim and culprit, hangman too,
All in one, here go you.

About the groundlessness go spin,
Who bear no grudge and hear no sin.
Become the Self itself shall judge.

THE DAUGHTER THOUGHT

King Acrisius, being warned that he would die by the hand of his daughter's son, imprisoned Danae in a Tower of Brass *inaccessible to all men. But Zeus visited her; and Perseus, who was set adrift on the sea at his birth, and preserved through many adventures, came at last unknown before King Acrisius at Argos. There in the games, his cast so far outflew all others that the discus fell on the King's instep and killed him.*

Walled up, walled in, the maiden doom
   The King, her father, dares not kill;
   Ruefully subject to his will,
Secure, he thinks, as his own tomb.

But, but within all let or lour,
   There rules an order without bound:
   Cyclic, unsearchable, but found
When the unthinkable junctures flower.

And startling as the fore-felt rime
   The sense resists and would refuse
   Justly and when it's due to lose
The step denied steps in in time.

Welcome as wind-borne pollen shower
   The Cloud-bringer—O clouds unfurl!—
   Comes in upon the waiting girl
And puts to shame that Brazen Tower.

The Golden Shower; the Virgin Birth;
   The Infant Voyage: what Moses in you all
   But draws his power thence? his Call
Clearer; firmer his title to the Earth.

Acrisius you! That daughter thought
   The King in you would still confine
   In loth foreknowledge from her line
Will come your deathblow—as it ought.

Be welcome, unknown shoot of ours,
   Before our footstool when you stand.
   Here is the discus to your hand:
To the casting line! Run out the hours!

NONE CAN TELL

Welcome the Fool's own Cap,
The stuffed and prick't-up Ear,
All-hail each hissing Bell,
Caper and Crow and Leer!
From now on, what I mean to mean,
From now on, none can tell,
　　No one can tell.

Bless those Behaviourists
Who made us out all *Jack*
(*a-Lantern & o'clock*)
Our only Wear, Good-lack!
—Benefit of Clergy now being out—
To save us in the Dock.

Here's to old Flesh and Blood
That do so deep deceive
Heaven and Earth and Hell!
Beauty's Eyes you do believe
Though what their Tears or Smiles can prove
Why none, no, none can tell,
　　No one can tell.

Cunninger still the Verse
When with its ruddering Rime
From perjured Breath it wrings
Sincerity sublime.
You'd think a Poet had an End
In View in what he sings.

So then, in what I write,
Look! Look not for me.
My Lines will do as well,
Let them as well go free;
They say whatever they chance to say
And what more none can tell,
　　No, none can tell.

HARVARD YARD IN APRIL:
APRIL IN HARVARD YARD

To and fro
Across the fretted snow
Figures, footprints, shadows go.

Their python boughs a-sway
The fountain elms cascade
In swinging lattices of shade
Where this or that or the other thought
Might perch and rest.
              And rest they ought
For poise or reach.
Not all is timely. See, the beech,
In frosty elephantine skin
Still winter-sealed, will not begin
Though silt the alleys hour on hour
Débris of the fallen flower,
And other flowery allure
Lounge sunlit on the Steps and there
Degrees of loneliness confer.

Lest, lest . . . away!
You may
Be lost by May.

MAGNOLIA HOUR

Brimful of abandoned hope
These silver trees will sail
Their sudden crowding fleet aloft:
Then gaily on the gale
They'll spill the wreckage down the slope.

Heartfelt our faltering glance
Catches the flash and fall.
No Will-you—Won't-you paltering there!
'All *out*, no *in*!' The call
Could tempt a heart to join that dance.

No, no, old snowflake thought!
Whatever you still must do,
Or say, or be, has still its right.
That flaunt is not for you,
Who, in an ampler gamble caught,
Live with a doubtfuller end in sight.

TO DUMB FORGETFULNESS

Forget, forget . . . Forget what you forget.
The diary entry: name, fact, place and date
Let go and let the loitering dead be dead.

Missed cue, lost quote, worst muddled figures yet,
The choice statistic, much mislaid of late,
Forget, forget . . . Forget what you forget.

The side-long glance, the sigh, the oblique head,
The lifeless tone you could anticipate
Let go and let the loitering dead be dead.

The hidden face, the word too gently said
That spelled maybe a formula of fate
Forget, forget . . . Forget what you forget.

Why should they haunt you, hold you in their debt,
Remind you of their loss? The debt is paid.
Let go and let the loitering dead be dead.

All feeling now like foliage to be shed.
Did you forget regret as well must fade?
Let go and let the loitering dead be dead.
Forget, forget . . . Forget what you forget.

TRINITY BRETHREN ATTEND

There was a young fellow went by:
Alight his eye
And his step was free.
But what could he see?
What could he be?
Ah, me!

Here's an old buffer drawn near:
Oh, dear,
Do what he will
He sees less still!

In between:
The man,
Firm and cool:
Their measure and their mean:
Green
And a fool.

Any day now
When all is said and done
The three
Will be
One
With Niniveh
And Tyre and Babylon;
As—in a different way,
But who knows how?—
They
Under their
Self-same star
Were
And are.

DISMISSION

Farewell, young Muse! you've teased me long enough,
Promising lines and rimes you didn't furnish.
You claimed you had some public's ear as well.
You've pestered me to clip and file and burnish
But rust adorns, I find, and dust's the stuff.

You've lectured me on What and How and Why
Until there's not a theme I care to touch.
Artful and heartless, innocent and sly
Go decorate some other poet's couch
Now all is almost over. Here! Goodbye!

Go wrench his sense and regulate his voice.
Tell him there's nothing left for verse to say
Though only you can find the way to say it.
Give him my greeting with your rates of pay
And never let him know he has no choice.

TO BE

Still missing it though:
Though what, none know.
Still journeying on:
On what commission?
Still hoping to be There
Ere we Be anywhere;
And waiting till an Hour
Our idleness empower:
For Place and Hour and We
We seek at best to be
Being a-want, all three
And indiscernably.

BIRTHDAY THOUGHTS

Surely this Day
May beg forbearance
Both of and for
Forbears and descendants.

Summon I dare
Heirs and legators:
Each day—but two—both:
Loth mediators.

Forbear days! You
Through whom I'm here
Handing along our
Powers and our fear,

How may a moment,
In t'motley dressed,
Hint, when forgot,
What might be best?

Predecessors (take heed)
Need no more be dead
Than successors succeed:
Seed ill-sped.

Most children don't now
Bow much to parents.
Most famous men
End up as defendants.

Pledging the future,
Your careless abandon
Squandered the wherewithal
All could now stand on.

Wide off the beam,
Dream confounded,
Seeing no more than I
Why we weren't grounded,

You ruined me
Betimes. Much, much as I,
I, in my turn
Burn what   they'd live by.

Must such be the fashion
(Passion gone sour)
What the movement decrees
Lees of our hour?

Would that all together
Whether this needs be
We might consider
Iteratively!

Since on a Birthday
May a new Day start;
An old lag lapse
Perhaps; *Revenant* depart!

MANIFOLD MOTION

Philosophers ador'd the Night, accounting it to have some great Mystery and Deity in it.—Peter Sterry

Taught, for a moment, by discomfiture,
Gave up and took the treasure to the dump.
Found then, the drainage had to foul the pump.
Give up! Clear out! One endless overture!

Every arrival this; and every departure:
Leaping from rotting strength to iron stump,
With all at stake in each blindfolding jump.
Home-coming this: lighting out at a venture.

Twirl'd up aloft in limitless endeavour
To be sunk back, as soon, below the least.
Caught between choices scissor-set to sever
The toiling thread. From that cocoon released,
Firefly headlighted to annul whatever
Night I flit through: ignorant as a priest.

FELLOW FEELING

More than affectionately old,
Old clock,
With staid tick-tock,
Blocking out, rounding up
The intangible flow;
Warming-pan pendulum
Sedately swaying;
Minute hand stepping and staying,
Acting, enacting,
Again and ago . . .
After faint hum
You strike:
One. Endless the wait before . . .
Two. But this I especially like:
Three comes sooner and the rest come
Quicker and quicker till the sum
Is told.

Coconut Grove, Florida
10 February 1959

END OF A COURSE

In Memory of Theodore Spencer:
4 July 1902—18 January 1949

He and I,
Giving Humanities I together,
Iliad, Old Testament, Phaedo . . . I,
New Testament, Paradiso, Hamlet . . . he,
Strolled to my room through the open weather.
Full January thaw. Examination weighed,
He turned to go: 'The readiness is all!'
Said to the Calendar on the wall,
Stooping to glance at it to see
The date in Spring when we'd be free.
'Earlier than ever!' Rubbing his hands in glee,
Leapt down my steps into the sun.

All done.
He crossed the Yard, waved to a friend,
Looked up a book, then took
A taxi-ride that had no end.

Coconut Grove, Florida
18 January 1959

44

HOPE

To D. E. P. in hospital for a broken hip

My dear: Wales has a slab
Named Hope—a tall, buff, tilting thing.
It listens, these late centuries,
To querulous, lost, impatient lambs
And the ambiguous sheep
Conversing through the mist.
There, leading, one cool Spring,
Rope out, the holds glare ice,
You found your pocket scissors:
                              stab by stab
Picked enough clear, floated on up.
                         I keep
A memory of that for other jams:
You immaterialist,
Who know when to persist.

Recall the Epicoun:
Night, welling up so soon,
Near sank us in soft snow.
At the stiff-frozen dawn,
When Time had ceased to flow,
—The glacier ledge our unmade bed—
I hear you through your yawn:
'Leaping crevasses in the dark,
That's how to live!' you said.
No room in that to hedge:
A razor's edge of a remark.

THE TEMPORAL THE ALL?

Yes, not less present now than when
You gambolled down that slope,
Shuffling the beech-
Leaves,
Kicking up such a din
We had to talk or walk.

But now is here, and then was then.

Even a dead beech-
Leaf,
Within its javelin head, can glow
As warmly as a peach.

There, there!
It's but a skin,
A skin, a bloom,
So thin it leaves
No room for grief.

Tricks of the visible,
Its sunset show.

From
The Indivisible
All come. And we,
Before the senses were
And after their despair,
Are what no eye can see.

COURT OF APPEAL

Nature is better dressed than Man.
These various Birds and Fish,
Even the 'gator on his bank,
Can
Make one wish
We people weren't so rank.

And, most, the Humbled One,
Self-fluent, living Stream,
Upon his belly in the dust:
None
Of all seem
In better Taste.

His suiting modest, rich, subdued,
Choice custom drape,
In stripe and weave correct:
Shrewd
For a Shape
So bitterly abject!

He, who originally rolled
'Erect', uplifted high
'His burnish't Neck of verdant
Gold',
'Crested aloft' and eye
Observant,

Through which the sight of Eve at work
Stooping amid her 'Flourie Plat',
Converting Satan, could
Irk
Evil itself, the Plot forgot:
'Stupidly good';

He whom the Tempter found
('Fearless unfeared he slept.'
Why should he watch unwarned?)
And,
Within him crept,
Seized and suborned:

Brer Serpent, never a fool,
'Nor nocent yet'—a friend
To all—how should he know?
Tool
Only and
Punished so!

See now, the fly, the bream,
Bass, cormorant, gar and 'gator
Ravening. Was this all through
Him?
And later
Bikinis too?

Everglades National Park
27 January 1959

NEAR THE STOVE

Lenin declared that Any Cook
   —How sure the hope that chose the word—
Ought to be able to govern the state.
   Did Lenin cook? I haven't heard.

Besides, what's cooking? Ham and eggs?
   The soufflé? *Pâté* Aphrodyne?
The accounts? Production curve reports?
   History? The party Line?

Seek nobler thoughts. Find Lenin's aim:
   To glorify the gifts of men.
Shut up the holocidal shop
   And call us to the banquet then!

RESIGN! RESIGN!

> Up hill, down dale . . .
> So ran the tale.

We have them in our bones:
Ten thousand miles of stones,
Moraine, débris and scree;
As many, could-be twice,
Over the fissured ice,
The clinging, slippery snows
That of our feet dispose;
As many again, or more,
Beside the torrent's roar,
Within the scented gloom
Or through the sorrowing cwm.

Or by the scythe-worn dell,
And cow-placated swell
Up the redeeming grass
Lifting toward the pass.

Along the ridge itself,
The ridge that earns its pride,
Riven from either side:
Lord of the rift or shelf
Whence the awaiting cliffs
Hang out their 'buts' and 'ifs'
To magnetize the eye
From sweeping round the suspect sky,
That could so soon prevent
Our inexplicable intent.

Or where the driven snow
Invites our steps to show
No fluted, rearing wall,
Or plum'd crest too tall
For our impertinence.

What did we gather thence?
The bootprint in the dust,
The upward roll and thrust,
The limber footfall plunging down,
The axe-head friendly in the palm
Or snug between the sack and arm.
Clutches of delicate fears,
Qualms as the *néant* nears:
Relieved—our summit joys;
Relived—what toys!

All that—Goodbye!
And this has told you why:
Not of all that bereft,
But we, ourselves, have left . . .
Leave that behind.
And not as Fall . . .
Even resigned.

SATIATION THEORY

I.

After the great wave lesser waves seem shrunk
To some; to others not. Back here in the womb,
Here in our nearest mock-up, we assume
Under deficiency of waves we're sunk
And kick to be let out. Accordingly:
Those take pain best who shrink fresh waves the most;
Those make best prisoners whose waves least have lost
After—because of—what wild ecstasy?

The extravert, they say, will underrate:
His but to DO—not cultivate the sigh.
Those who grow old with grace don't like life less.
The escape from love's for the smart satiate.
If we might choose, it seems the choice would lie
Between a dodge with pain—and loneliness.

II.

Slung like a spider's web above a void
—Image of frailty, stronger though than steel—
Strings, these, for every pang that you can feel,
For all the tastes in you that can be cloyed.
Tauten or slacken for the testing touch.
Hereabouts the mean is; seek it heedfully,
While a remainder answers faithfully.
Enough's enough; too much can be too much.

Listen! The astonished ear scales down its take.
Look! The insulted eye declines, won't see
As formerly it could. Be not so rough;
Let not your will its own attunement break,
Nor strain the joints of thought; but skilfully
Salute *Enough*. Little enough's *Enough*.

III.

To what excess you practice what you preach!
A poem can glut or starve. Starve too far,
Pump down too low a vacuum, there you are:
Met by a change of sign. You overreach.
What was too little has become too much,
The want itself has swollen out of bounds,
The silence grown too loud. The change confounds
Presence and absence: they wring you in one clutch.

Living's at least a poem it must dictate:
No cancelling, nor known what it's about:
It balances between Within - Without
Across ten billion axes.   Satiate?
What's been controls how we may take what comes.
Pray, fingers, pray: 'Let us not be all thumbs!'

SUCCESS

Of a Promising Student, in Anticipation

A world deep in his debt
Pays interest full—and yet . . .

What need was solaced so?
What lonely fight,
What sacrifices of delight,
What anguish in the long ago?

And what extremities of prayer
Built up what head of longing there,
What hunger for renown
That now he must disown
With apprehensive frown?

And what wry self-distrust
The young hood-winker thrust
Into such coy pursuit?
What bittering snub
Was just enough to stub
And polish such astute
Appraisal of the ropes
That realize such hopes?

By what adroit disguise
Grained in beyond surprise
Did this suave metamorph
This migrant on a whorf
This psyche out of grub,
This pard attired as hind
Leave all the rest behind?

                    Little sign
Amid such high, benign

Complacency and charm,
Such calm array;
But some quick anger and alarm
Peeking through the bland display
And the alerted eye,
Spying out who deny.

SILENCES

The Talipot Palm of Ceylon, one of the wonders of the plant world, grows to be 80 feet high in 40 years, then flowers, producing 2 tons of bloom and thousands of fruits. It then dies.—*Notice under a photograph in the David Fairchild Tropical Gardens, Coconut Grove, Florida*

I.
Suppose we meet a silence. While it's clear,
While not a wave checks in along the shore,
While nothing breaks it, not a thought or word,
Not a leaf stirring—where will we be then?

Is it that silence you would choose to hear?
Or our own selves thinking? Ours the floor
Our own selves all the audience: to be heard,
To hear—beyond the reach of men?

Silence, no doubt, 's the ground of utterance,
Pausing its pulses and completing it;
No utterance without. But listen! When,
If ever in the windings of the dance,
To-be-said and *saying* in perfection fit,
Another silence listens: listen again.

II.

The outcome's not the point, those sportsmen say.
The over-all outcome's something else again.
Our outcome, what we've hoped so to achieve,
Could not have been, or done, as we supposed—
Suppose it somehow realized.   We play
Our games; win, lose.   All which would be inane
If even   the uttermost we may conceive
Of less conditional enclosing games   forclosed
A thing.   How ask all that to freeze
An instant and for what! That we may succeed?
In what?   In due accordance with the Way?
In being ourselves? In doing what we please?
In getting but an inkling of our need?
In learning how to hold our peace or pray?

III.

For all such fleetings—figures on a ground—
Let the Giraffe play emblem: none so tall,
Gentle, aloof, free, delicate and calm;
He bears the casting net set in his skin;
Strides like a wave, within those meshes bound;
Lives there unspotted, Captive of the All.
Another image shape: the Talipot Palm
Ending itself for others to begin.

Take and make over. There's no soon or late
In the perpetual. This would still have been
Had our concern kept concert with our powers.
Ground becomes figure: what we would create
Backs down, fades out, gives place to what's between
The lines, the patches; and behind the hours.

SUNRISE

All brightens swiftly; all will soon be clear.
The little lights have vanished, star by star;
Along this shore lingers but Lucifer.
Clear: we were never where we saw we were,
Nor are, nor will be, where we see we are;
Nor far off from it, either; no, nor near.

    You make broad day your house;
My mind moves with the bat, the owl, the mouse.

Turn and, in turning, know what's turned about;
What turns you too: the handled and the hand.
Being become the most elaborate top,
(Bare earth's the oldest, simplest, in the shop)
Topmost, we say, who the most understand,
Go spin your yarn beyond the doughtiest doubt.

    What's truest should be right;
This beaver industry befits the night.

To spin a clue you do not stand your ground,
Unless that ground's the axis of the spin;
But axes have their cyclic wobbles all,
(The Pole Star wanders, is precessional)
Distinctive vortices worked out within
—Mounted, you say, upon—the daily round.

    You make broad day your house;
My mind moves with the bat, the owl, the mouse.

My wobble now salutes your wobble, you;
Yet let's not inconsiderately rejoice
In individualities we gain
(Thus to subvert our only suzerain)
By random shrinkage of our scope of choice
Or deprivation of our orbits' due.

What's truest should be right;
This beaver industry befits the night.

Broad day shows more than you may care to see.
It is the night sky opens to the stars.
We obscurantists can pretend, as well.
(Baillie! Where are you off to with that bell!)
More light! And more! Forever! Naught debars
Fact breeding on — on to infinity.

You make broad day your house;
My mind moves with the bat, the owl, the mouse.

Dam up a rivulet to form a pond,
The water well above the lintel mark,
And build within a wolverine-proof Lodge.
(The underwater doorway is the dodge.)
There, as day dazzles, you preserve your dark.
Nibble your store of bark. Let be beyond.

What's truest should be right;
This beaver industry befits the night.

BY THE POOL

*In his meditation under the Bo tree, Gotama may have decided—in
love and pity—to teach a doctrine which would do men good rather
than another doctrine which few only could follow.*

Not beneath the Bo tree
—Its long-tongued leaves
Poplar-like, a-flutter—
This Buddha sits;
But by a limpid water
Welling by;

Which maybe more befits
Words none will utter
Whoever sigh.

There search-winds of heaven
Twirl an imploring leaf,
Set the whole Tree a-shiver
In glory, in grief:
Beneath, the All-giver
In pity willed
To bind up the Sheaf.

Here by his River
That tumult's stilled.

*Not ours to bind,
That way the sword;
Who lay aside the cord
They alone find.*

Truly inaudible
—Yet to be heard
By the ear of the mind—
The penultimate word
Ultimate ripple.

The still figure
Beyond the flow
Listens, listened
Aeons ago.
Ever a-flutter
Must all words be.

Here is an end.

from FURTHER POEMS (1960-1970)

ALASKAN MEANDER

Flying this low, below that river bed
   There shows another, another under that,
   Palimpsest meanderings outspread.

Horizon-wide, the piedmont falls so flat
   The streams can wander—freely, we might say.
   Cut where they will, spill over, twine and plait,

Explore, essay, renege, revert or play
   What ox-bow games they please; lick at a bank,
   Silt up a channel; anyway, have their way.

Not so at all. We've something else to thank!
   All streams in sight in parallel have told
   A common story; it was the West that sank

Tilting all beds together; each stream rolled
   The way it had to. East and West in turn
   Sway—see-saw—up and down. All flow's controlled.

The whole world wiggles; wriggle we must and learn
   How the earthwave within us bulges by,
   Troughs us or hoists, whichever way we yearn.

Not harsh or crabbed, as dull schools imply,
   But queer beyond all that, we may discern,
   Beyond our like or loathing, grin or sigh,

     How daunting is divine autonomy.

CONDITIONAL

Beckon some cragsman's paradise from the sky,
Heart-beat slows down, lungs halt their heave,
So to descry, conceive
How it was with me when that sport began:
Muscle and nerve wrought for me by the strain.
Fain as of old I feign that yet I can.

Pass by some image of the world's desire,
Eye beam narrows, glance sharpens to discern,
So to attire, adorn
Some visitant from when that hunt began
Whose hardihood now tells me what is vain.
Fain as of old why feign that yet I can?

Butterfly thought, sail gaily through the void,
Seeking your mate, belike—gale-borne astray,
To be destroyed, betray,
Ice-caught, the thoughts from which your life began:
Torn downy wings that will not sail again.
Fain as of old, I feign that yet I can.

WAKING THOUGHTS

Turn the mind then to that
Which being won all's done.
Stable it there
To take that rest as best.
Too many the mind's roads,
Their throngs too beat, too fleet,
Too unaware.
Mind is its bonds
And they'll not break.
      How wake?

Wake! Why, I'm wide awake,
Feel, think as though I know.
Or, is it, knew?
Know, knew it: what I'm not
And what I have to do
Both when and now. But how?
Being beyond my mind
Yet with a bond to keep,
I've both to find
      And sleep.

Out of the ancient flux
Poised here to chart some part,
I note the alternates
Mutual as mates:
The nights and days, and praise
How the clear eye, our sky,
Must cloud and close,
Wear out as sieve;
That others live
      Must die.

Should what I would chart here
Come to seem plain, how vain,
Inept, absurd!

What's it about but doubt?
As if a word
Could be, without
An utterance, heard
Or hearer hear
Save in some subduing
        Of din.

What a word means who'd say
Will new words choose and use;
What these in turn may mean
Invites a new to-do.
And so on . . . please.
But when the sense is seen,
What then has been,
What's clear in that serene,
What seeing is
        Who sees?

To say now what I know
About my send and end:
Rudder'd I am and sail'd,
Can set a course, enforce,
Amend, subvert, rebel.
That's mutiny, for we
Life-long are all at sea;
Captaining it
As our ghostly crew
        See fit.

Not, by a sight, by chance.
As we begin there's in
Us, unconceived, our plan;
We've each our bent; are sent
To show what comes of that;
In such self-government must ask,
Cell ask of cell, 'What's well?'

But to pursue
      Our task.

Its end? What but to probe:
Record, prepare, bear, share . . .
That the design may grow
Worth even its cost.
The lost, they show
Us what we're for.
We but relay. What more?
What further care?
      You say.

AWAITED

No heron, swung
Squint-eyed
Above its tide,
Full-strung
To dart,
Is more alert:
    Stir in a reed,
    Horizon head,
    Flaw in the flood . . .
At once, wide wings abroad
He's up
Away.
Who prey are prey.

So I
Minding my step
And sky,
Where any air
Can scare me from
My nearer aim;
Where the unknown
    Controls the scene
    Stages the show,
    The persons too . . .
Writes all anew
To ask me: Who
The playwright is?
Whose prey are you?
What sort of game
With thing or thought
Could be your own?

What 'gator now
    Below, behind . . .
    Within your mind . . .
Some predator,

Shadow of harm,
With what swift fright
Shakes you to flight,
Makes you let swim
The fish in sight,
Flap off, alight
From brief survey
Elsewhere; there stay
While it's your whim
Or till some
Fresh alarm?

Here on this strand,
With what would do
Well within thrust,
You wait. You trust.
May your fish too
Be trustful! And
May those who wait
For you!
This is your Fate:
Not soon or late,
But ever;
Minute by minute
In it.

WAYMARK

Built me up duly
To seem what I should:
Guide for all comers;
Stoneman beyond
Winters and summers,
Cannot and could;
Steadfast, in bond,
Shafted secure,
With a crest of bright quartz
To sharpen the lure.

Links in a chain
Should stonemen be,
Each man again
His next men see
Upholding plain
Joint guarantee
For one bent whither
And him bound thence
And you won hither
None may know whence:
Servants, escorts,
Companions, defence.

Not stand alone
Only its own
Answerless stone.

Knowing no neighbour,
Distant or near,
Sharing no labour;
Dutyless here.
Though as his duty,
As for that sent,
In that spent,
Bearing the blame,

But as his duty
One came,
Built me up truly,
Built me
And went.

Built me up duly
To seem . . .

THE EDDYING FORD (*Genesis, 32*)

JACOB:
    Go, servants, seek Lord Esau out
        High in the land of Seir,
    'Let now Lord Esau know no doubt
        If Jacob now draw near.'

    And further say: 'These twenty years
        In Laban's house he stayed
    For gain to calm Lord Esau's fears;
        And be no more afraid.

    And oxen, asses, rams and ewes
        He has for thy delight,
    And sends us now to bear this news . . .
        To find grace in thy sight.'

NARRATOR:
    To Esau came these servants then
        Bowing unto the ground:
ESAU:
    'Whose?'
SERVANTS:
        'Thy servant Jacob's men.'
NARRATOR:
    Then Esau grimly frowned.

ESAU:
    'Go tell that double-crossing ape,
        That birthright-buying cat,
    This next time he will not escape.'
NARRATOR:
        And as he spake he spat.

ESAU:
    'Pottage, yes and savoury meat,
        The hairy neck and hands!
    Go tell that smoothy let his feet
        Not step into my lands.

    Or blessings shall he get from me
        The blessings of the sword,
    For him and his. Sands of the sea!
        Beyond the eddying ford!'

NARRATOR: So sped, those servants came again
        Saying:
SERVANTS: 'Here Esau comes
    And with him come four hundred men
        With spears and swords and drums.'

NARRATOR: Then greatly Jacob grew afraid
        Lest Esau from his wild
    Come down and slaughter man and maid,
        The mother with the child.

To appease such brotherly amity
    Two hundred ewes and rams,
Two hundred goats, both he- and she-,
    And camel colts and dams

He gave into his servants' hands
    To go forth, drove by drove,
Grazing across Lord Esau's lands
    To be his luck and trove,

And straitly charged each servant now:
JACOB: 'When Esau meeteth thee,
And asketh: "Whence and whose art thou?"
    Thus shall thine answer be:

"Thy servant Jacob's are we all
    —May we be to thy mind!—
And others follow at thy call,
    And he, he comes behind." '

RACHEL: Help us, O Teraphim I stole,
    When we bow before this Lord!
JACOB: O FEAR of Isaac, may this toll
    Save *Joseph* from the sword!

O FEAR, deliver even me
    From my brother's angry hands!

> Surely, Thou said'st, shall thy seed be
>   As the sea's unnumbered sands.

NARRATOR: So flock by flock his presents passed,
        Well-spaced, across the ford;
    Then wives and offspring, Joseph last,
        To shield him from the sword.

    And Jacob stayed and was alone
        Before the ford that night.
JACOB: What more have I that is my own
        To give or hold by right?

THE EL: Thyself.
JACOB: And what art thou?
THE EL: Thyself.
JACOB: Wrestle thou then with me!
THE EL: Myself to overcome Myself
        Will wrestle here with thee.

JACOB: What art thou but this eddying ford
        By which I sent across,
    To save me from my brother's sword,
        My winnings and my loss.

THE EL: And thou too art this eddying ford
        By which were sent across
    To save thee from thy brother's sword:
        Those winnings and that loss.

JACOB: Long is this night we wrestle out,
        Yet dayspring draweth nigh,
    Foul-handled though I be this bout
        In the hollow of my thigh.

THE EL: Let go! Day breaketh on the sky!
        Day breaketh! Let me go!

JACOB: Yet shalt thou bless me from on high
    Or e'er I let thee go.

THE EL: By what name?
JACOB: Jacob.
THE EL: Now be given
    Thy new name Israel:
    God striveth. Who with God hath striven
    O'er men shall he prevail.

JACOB: And thy name? Thine? I pray thee, thine?
THE AL: Why dare'st thou ask my name?
    Yet do I bless thee. And the sign
    Shall this be: thou art lame.

NARRATOR: And Jacob called by name the place
    Peniel: *The Face of God*.
JACOB: For here have I seen God face to face
    Yet onward yet I plod.

NARRATOR: And lifting up his eyes he saw,
    As he limped along again,
    Under the risen sun, Esau
    And his four-hundred men.

POSADA

For reading by groups, during the ten days before Christmas. Through this period, it is the custom in Oaxaca, Mexico, for friends to pay evening calls upon one another. They expect to have to knock loud and long before they are admitted. They are enacting Joseph's harrowing appeals.

Around the churches at sundown companies of clamant, excited children batter on firmly closed doors; within, companies of equally clamant children refuse them admittance. All the doors of the church are besieged in turn by the chanting procession. Finally, there is a grand climax. All doors are opened and there is candy galore for all.

This little play tries to combine after-sunset arrivals at many village inns in remote desert landscapes with the pre-Christmas drama.

MARY: Go Joseph knock! O knock again!
              Again knock on the Door!

SATAN: That this all-labouring world of pain
              Need travel on no more.

GABRIEL: That what will be may be
          And what must be can be
          That what could be should be.

MARY: Yet, yet, again! Knock on again!
              Again knock on the Door!

SATAN: That this nigh-foundering race of men
              Learn what the sword is for.

JOSEPH: So I, despairing, hammer on my heart.
          O open, open wide and let blow in
       The unsparing Word that chose me for this part
          Filling this void that's hunger and that's sin.

PORTER: Knock at this hour! Be off, you there!
              Why should we find you room!

No opening now, for pay nor prayer.
 Think you're the crack of doom!

They come by day the folk that we let in
 To take their ease, for light and food and sleep.
This Door won't open now for all your din.
 An Inn's an Inn and not a fortress keep.

INNKEEPER: This night's not like another night.
 Some THING's abroad I doubt.
My porter there is in the right
 To keep these vagrants out.

GUEST IN
THE INN: Slow and cold, dust blowing all the way:
 Wind-burn parched and foot and saddle sore.
A ruinous place but still a place to stay.
 What's all that argie-bargie at the Door?

ANOTHER
GUEST: Snug here! Let's hope those batterings at the
           Door
 Don't mean the You Know Who have caught
           us up!
I had as lief not fight it out once more.
 Meanwhile we may as well fill up the cup.

SERVING
WENCH: A pinchy lot to serve their meat and drink,
 Smile at, be saucy with—and sometimes more:
At beck and call to any nod or wink.
 Ah, that young lad so haggard at the Door.

ANOTHER
GUEST: Good pickings maybe. No pig in a poke.
 Some chance, at least, to see which of them's
           which.
Who wants to waste his talents on the broke?
 So here's our bumper toast: 'God Save the
           Rich!'

ANOTHER
GUEST: It's just as well we left the pearls behind.
         Don't too much like the looks of some of
                      these.
      Better not seem to have it on your mind.
         These gentry's style in arguing isn't 'Please!'

ANOTHER
GUEST: Stoney the waste and blinding chill the wind,
         Secretive and hid the passers-by.
      Men get more talkative when they have dined
         Grow less inclined to take you for a spy.

JOSEPH: What Inn is this? So pitiless its Door,
         It will not hark or heed
      It will not hear however I implore
         It will not even let me show the Need.

      O more than life to me, so not my life;
         Why you, all this on you be laid,
      O my betrothed, my partner not my wife?
         What doom is this set on an honest maid?

FIRST
NEIGHBOUR: She looks too good to be in such a plight;
         Demure yet proud. Uppish, no doubt.
      But now she comes to learn what serves her
                     right:
         In such a night as this to be shut out!

SECOND
NEIGHBOUR: Nothing but riff-raff, flotsam of the Ways.
         Improvident and feckless are the poor!
      Without the wit even to count the days!
         Then go and knock on any decent door!

DONKEY: Hee-haw! See-saw! She's had her fun and fling!
         And now it's all caught up with her at last,
      She must have been the doxy of a King;
         Not that poor chap so helpless and aghast.

SATAN: Here is my cue to play the Morning Star!
          Too big she is to weather out the night.
     I'll show them where the hay and manger are.
          Follow me now, all Glory and all Might.

GABRIEL: Helpful as ever the Adversary is,
          Alert to forward what he calls his plan.
     The very first to think he knows what's his,
          Acting his part out between God and man.

       That what will be may be
       And what must be can be
       That what could be should be

FUTURE INTIMATIVE

Look forward lightly. No news ever yet
Could be as good or bad as it appear.
Don't cross the sundering flood before it's here,
Getting all set to meet what mayn't be met.

It's coming; yes, of course. But what will come?
What no one knows—so, flutterling, be still.
Go make your bed and glance up at the hill.
The hill's the whence, although the hope be mum.

Making the bed, what fleeting tremor's shed,
As 'twere an echo of an inner laughter;
A scent, fore-sending, of a follow-after?
Look forward lightly yet and make your bed.

SLEEPLESS

Under-worry one:
What's done is done;
Leave ill alone!

Weary wonder two:
What could I do
Hearing them all:
Call against call?

Why, I could weep!

On-coming trouble three:
Hamlet's, Cuchulain's sea.

Reap as I've sown?

Throw up the sponge?

Before it fall
Into what sweet deep
Waters of sleep
Do I plunge

RELAXED TERZA RIMA

For Marianne Moore

On taking on a more rational order of being

Say to her, 'Do',
As is your wont,
You. Who are you?

What do you want
Clipping away
With 'do' and with 'don't',
With 'can' and with 'can't',
'Will you' and 'won't'?

Psyche, we say,
Feminine, she.
She? Who is she,
Standing at bay,
When we say to her 'shan't'?

On taking on?
'On' means *about*
And *about to*, too,
Having so done,
And *having to do*,
As well as, no doubt,
That being won!

More rational, yes,
But who's to choose?
Is it a dress
Psyche must wear,
Trying it on,
Letting it out,
Taking it in?

Try out a guess
At what 'it' 's at there,
Neat as a pin.
Lip-loads of 'em
Constrain a grin.

Trying what on?
A season's wear?
Letting what out?
Not only 'where?'
Taking who in?

So with orderliness.
None would condemn
What the deceptious
Do with a hem.

Conscientious
Folk, though, claim
That to look alright
Isn't all our aim;
That shining bright
Isn't the same,
As yet, for us,
As being alight
With the gem-like flame;
That we are not yet quite
Without use for shame.
Our thanks to them;
No animus.

SOLITUDE

Where are you going to, my witty maid,
    And, what may your true name be?
Psyche's my name, kind sir, she said,
    Curtseying comelily.

Psyche, you know what risks you run
    Here all alone, said he.
Risks all alone, gay sir, there are none.
    Risks come from company.

Goddess you must be, Psyche dear,
    For beast you could never be.
And Aristotle has made it clear
    You've no other choice, said he.

One who would live to herself alone,
    And a beauty especially,
Must, it has often enough been shown,
    Be a brute or a deity.

Why yet, fond sir, try what you will,
    Alone I would ever be,
My own, my strange, companion still,
    Undesolatedly.

Poor Belial, were you still a soul,
    Or a soul could you ever see,
You'ld know why all who seek their goal
    Still journey lonelily.

ET EGO IN ARCADIA

Not much left now to prize: in gait,
In posture, contour, poise to rate:
Uncouthenings so thick of late
Slim the chance that they'll abate
While what's ensuing we await.
Ah well! Why cavil at one's fate?
 In Arcady the limbs are straight.

Nor much more scope for articulate
Comparings of the great with great;
And filterings out of scorn and hate;
Compassionate eyeing of the counterfeit.
Frustration's still our true estate.
Ah well! Why quarrel with the date?
 In Arcady ideals create.

FINHAUT

(Highest point on the railway over from Martigny to the French
frontier at Le Châtelard.)

An ominous name? Could be:
These gyring rails must mount no higher,
Firmly descend into another country.

Their duty's done. What though
Across the numinous gulf uprear
Sheer spires and sunlit snow;

Along this ravining brink
Our wheels will wind their squeal;
Tunnel to trestle to tunnel blink

On down, past footways to
Known heights now out of reach;
To this pass come, and through:

Who, sixty-odd years ago,
Happened here first to lift
My young mere eyes to snow.

NEW POEMS 1971-1977

'DEAR MEMORY'

Dear Memory,
   Oldest, closest, kindest Friend,
   Ever more faithful to the end.
     But not
   In bringing back
   What I think I lack:
   Facts, figures, places,
   Names and faces . . .
   And all the rest.
   Not so,
   But because you know
   What's best
     Forgot.

ANNUAL CLUB DINNER

Even as clouds float on to hidden ends
   So do these *convives* here converse together,
Each spending smiles reconstituting friends,
   While sighing at another's shortening tether.

Ambitions high and wide enough in scope,
   Shrunk in now to the promptings of the 'Double',
Here husband some late modicum of hope,
   Stumble across but too well-gleaned a stubble.

What was takes over, calls itself a Will:
   The fleeting eddy would the Tide forget
(The emptying soul, the unrelenting chill)
   And hold things as they were, yes, even yet.

Now does compassion, heart's eye, the unbidden,
Find for itself what in these clouds is hidden.

ANGLERS

Upon these banks in peace they sit
Well wrapt, close sheltered from the breeze
That blurs their waters' images;
They alone know what cares they've quit,
Designedly aloof, and tranquilly,
Silently, watching their lives float by.

Now, as they will, may they speculate:
So may they catch (so caught) the FISH
That could consume their every wish.
Within that deepening gloom may lurk
The more-than-Pike whose ancient power
Shall all that swims in time devour;
The wolf that, circling near, will sweep
In as the doom of all their sheep:
Their minutes, counted ere they hatch.

Or fable how, though none know whence,
Another Angler may let fall
Some secret Hook, hid in what bait
Inviting all. There let it wait.
Who gulps it down, who dares to snatch,
Aloft he goes without recall,
Departed hence to none know where.

You cunning ones, with your sly gear,
You but enact through your pretence
The all but universal fate,
O, anglers all, frequenting here.

Yet most, may sanity aver,
Who fish are as intent upon
Endearing duck, patrolling swan,
Willows every breath will stir,
Quietude deaf ear can hear:
Solacings though the turmoil near.

LONE GOOSE

Along this bank this goose
Waddles about,
Bandy-legged, heavy and stiff,
Pensive and grave, as if
Some major scheme were hatching.

With gull and duck and swan,
Seemingly watching,
On distant terms, if any,
She being alone, they many,
An active social throng.

Tired, as though resting off
After some long,
Hard flight; maybe astray;
Not sure if she should stay
Or go seek company.

Under her smooth-preen'd coat,
Effortlessly,
Her yellow beak she'll slip
Between her wings and sleep,
Save for one watchful eye
Alert to what comes now.

So I upon my bank,
Torn too by 'How?'
Explore my plight,
Rest off for other flight,
Slumbering all I may,
Unsure of my way out.

WINTER-FLOWERING PRUNUS

Not a bee left on the wing,
    Not even a fly
        Blown by;
Nor a bird yet come to sing,
Nor other glint of Spring.

This dauntless blossoming
    Flings out its rose-cheeked snow
        Its gauntlet resolute
            Defying *Time*
        For all who Him refute:
            Usurper *Time*
    Old Canceller, cancelled so.

This tree of trees
Twirling and tossing in the breeze
(Sheer emblem of His vagaries)
        Here bequeaths
        With these wild wreaths
    To those whose hearts are now
        Set on what *Time* denies
Their Everything.

        Frail *Time*;
    As *was*, with *is* and *shall be*, dies
        Poor *Time*;
Outwitted by a bough
        Or rime. . .

TALKING TO HIMSELF

'Morning never tries you till the afternoon.'
   So Kipling's 'Lullaby'. Not true for me.
      My dayspring all bewilderment, so slow
         Until noon toughened me to muddle through.

You will not say you learnt much, late or soon.
   That's not your way as even you'll agree,
      Except that you no more pretend to know
         What sort of ONE it is that talks to you.

One with whom to sup, you need that longer spoon?
   Or a celestial telling what to be?
      Or both in one together counselling so
         That you'll be less unready for what's due?
           Thus questioned, I
           May murmur in reply
         Time was when sunsets hurt. But now
         They hold my hand and tell me how.

ECCLESIASTICAL POLITY

Socrates: Be careful, Crito, and don't say anything you don't really believe . . . So reflect carefully. It is never right to return a wrong or to defend ourselves against wrong by threat of retaliation. You will agree to this or not?

Ten Protestants, off a bus, lined up and shot;
 Two days before, five Catholics much the same.
 Poor Churches, dragged back so to former shame,
Their lessons too well taught to be forgot.

Pity these murderers, victims committedly
 Of festering wrong. Before our world was built
 Its man-trap plan had foreordained our guilt:
That Accuser-Judge, that Heaven-promising Tree.

Eve's children still will need all 'forward wits',
 Their utmost skill in spiritual surgery,
 To clear these cankers, end this agony.

Beneath the Towers of Exeter yet sits
 Great Hooker on his throne, in gown and bonnet,
 An agate-eyed, yellow-legged seagull perched upon it.

ON THE PROSPECT OF MAN BECOMING HUMAN

    Of what now should we sing?
    Of Man's awakening,
Fulfilling him in wisdom and in power?
    By what remission,
    His absolution,
His unrepentant Heart must meet its Hour?
    By grace of his own past
    Forced now to what forecast?

    Too little to confess,
    Even in contriteness,
The slaughterings that won us our estate,
    The sly treacheries,
    Searing cruelties,
Foul entries in the chronicle of hate;
    The lurid litany,
    Summing our history.

    Led to profess that Love
    —All other Thrones above—
Was Man's sole choice to save himself from Man,
    Why wonder you that Fear
    Stepped in, instead, to steer
Our courses for us since our strife began,
    That wandering in that error
    We owe our lives to terror?

    Fear of, and for, Mankind
    Should light us back to Mind:
The All-threatening which could yet redeem;
    Should put away vain hopes
    And turn to that which gropes
Toward what is, show up the murder scheme,
    Grasp how we are misled
    Annihilate our dread.

Soul-breakingly too great
This burden of our fate
Until what we've begun bring in new hope
What do we to despond
Or account aught beyond
The searching reaches of our growing scope,
Till what we've learned to see
Will teach us how to be.

ENHEARTENMENT

Finest, least celebrated Human:
 the Chinese Woman.

See
 her lineless face,
 wide browed,
 quiet-eyed,
 held high,
 cheek curving in;
 lips silent
 eloquent;
 firm chin,
 braids sleek;
 a poise and grace
 by-passing our annoys,
 rebuking the world's noise.

Beyond despair
 what she,
 unbowed,
 can bear,
 dare, do
 and be.

THE PROPER STUDY

Know then thyself, presume not God to scan;
The proper study of mankind is man.

Pope, *Essay on Man*

Ignore thyself, and seek to know thy God.

Coleridge, *Self-knowledge*

Know, therefore, that thou art a god.

Cicero, *Scipio's Dream* (viii, 2)

Mindless the night, maybe,
That was and will be here,
And here's for ever
What must be most near.

Mindful, though memoryless,
Of the heretofore,
What should we but seek on,
Seek even to ignore?

Conceiving the pursued
Whatever name we lend,
Whatever guise it take,
Must be our source and end.

Thyself: how variant
The volatile soul can be!
Thy God: what presences,
Divined as variously!

While what these words
May mean is hit or miss,
The study proper
To us all is this.

May not these two quests be
At heart the same,
A single search misguided
By a double name?

The desolate aims
Through which the soul is sought
Are mirror-imaged
In the selves they've wrought.

So sacred mimers
For their dances dress,
As though possessed
By that they would possess.

The termless mysteries
Of knowing rest herein:
Who'ld know must be
Whence being did begin.

NOSCE TEIPSUM: IN HONOUR OF ALLEN TATE

Against that Hour, foreseen full-spent in sighings,
   Far earlier, when all seemed better than well,
Forebodings grown within through Time's denyings
   Taught even joys on their own ends to dwell,
   Thus readying themselves for what befell,
And husbanding their scope by such complyings
   As the inconstant world would then compel.

Alerted to the follies of defyings,
      His tyrant dreams now utterly declined,
        (Beyond conceit, gone, irrecoverably),
      Henceforth may he be to the rest resigned;
        Awake at last, detached, furnished to see;
      Axes all ground, tree-felling left behind,
        In calm abandonment content to be.

To be: What that may be let him disclose
   Who knows! Its mark at least, in Plato's plea,
'To act and to be acted on.' Suppose
   Neither without its other. Then no one free;
   Though happiest he whose life seems so to be,
Whose conduct from its inner nature flows
   As from wise laws within him—seemingly.

Least at the call of all that comes and goes,
      Ampler, more constant and considerate,
        The impulsions are that rule his commonweal.
      And when wounds ache from days once insensate
        May charity allay where Time can't heal.
      The thing most wanting to preserve this State:
        Tenting compassion for what men must feel.

Must feel: feeling's a vibrancy within a man,
   While laser thoughts cut and mould outwardly,
Swayed by, yet swaying feeling where they can,
   Forming and shaping all incessantly.

This Turtle and this Phoenix, thus they be:
Each source and end for both; since they began
  Mad and mistaken both, divisively.

A life: their footprints as they wrestling ran.
    Even so. Yet, by a Lot's wife look to learn,
      Learn both to know and feel their dual lour,
    Though tremblors shatter and the laser burn,
      By that, may SHOULD BE recollect its power,
    Grow masterly, by its own light return
      And be anew Itself . . . *against that Hour.*

CHANGE

After the event . . .
   This stillness.
      Emptiness.
         Vacancy.
            Absences.

            Defences
               gone
                   as though
               one
               had to learn
                     anew
     To be
          alone.
And then,
          as any rime must know,
these mountain
   waves,
             poised so,
               do
             show
            how to return,
assent,
remain,
            go
         on,
time and again,
since Time began,
   seeking what saves.

ESPIONAGE

And take upon's the mystery of things,
As if we were God's spies.

King Lear, V.iii.16

What daunted thoughts stand near
Unwilling to be heard,
Not bearing the unspoken
Though long unsecret word?

What may, what dare they dare,
Unwitting on what ground
Their thickshod feet may tread?
What's sought-for may be found.

DIVAGATION

> The intellect of man is forced to choose
> Perfection of the life or of the work.

W. B. Yeats

Who'ld think he'ld see so proud a Master blot
His copy-book so sadly?
Not
The intellect. That is no serf to force.
Ambitious rather, legendary source
Of all our error.
    Perfection? No.
That's not for us, however low
We pitch our aims.
  (Maybe the ants achieve it?)
For life and work
This conflict's but a lofty way to shirk.

  Speech this for a play:
  What some self-pitying poet well might say.

IN WANT

I.

What do, what should, I want?
   Whatever may
     Be my most inward eye
This knowledge grant!
   For this let me yet pray.

Grant this through which I long
   Effective power
     Over the thwart in me
To cure what's wrong
   And not but for an hour.

My wantings—all I lack—
   Constrain,
     Shroud up my inmost eye,
Shut in, hold back,
   Leave other seeing vain.

But this same ruling want—
   This strain,
     Being the core in me,
The source, the font—
   Could make me turn again.

II.

Of the soare faulcon so I learne to fly
                Spenser, 'An Hymne of Heavenlie Beautie', stanza 2.

Socrates told that wings
    Alone could show
       Whither and why to look
On those real things
Can teach us how to know.

Since then we've learnt to fly,
  Now understand
    How on a wing there forms
A void that grips the sky,
  As can henceforth be planned.

On this our planes depend
  And all air-foils,
    Socratic wings as well.
These wants have shaped our end
  Governed all chosen toils.

Whatever wings we watch
  They sail thereby:
    Hawk, seagull, soul or kite.
Who would some inkling catch
  Of us, look to the sky.

 III.
Then want must be your master.

Each want deftly supplies
  A growing need,
    Meets it continually.
And let not this surprise
  Since every venturing seed

That lives, divides and grows
  And comes to be
    Bearer of seed in turn
Through chains of wants arose,
  And inescapably.

Their wants they were; as we
  Are what we want.
    The rest the shadow is
That limns what we might be
  As *Can*'s defined by *Can't*.

So being comes about,
    Incomplete still,
        Of old, as now, and ever.
Beyond the reach of doubt
    Good finds its grounds in ill.

WHY

For Red Warren

O ye hypocrites, ye can discern the face of the sky, but can ye
not discern the signs of the times . . .

Matthew 16:3

Arise and do begin the day's adorning
That will complete the broad adorned day.

Hilaire Belloc

. . . While . . . far withdrawn,
God made Himself an awful rose of dawn

Tennyson

Not impious to ask
Why re-awaken?

Yet again
To watch that awful rose
The grey earth re-adorn?

Then re-dispose
Some lingering strength
To some old task;
Try to revive,
At length,
Some yet unshaken
Aim; regain
Or re-contrive
Some breath of morn
Reborn.

But stay! See: Shepherds' Warning!
Come night: Shepherds' Delight!

DITTY

The simples for this ditty
   Compound themselves in song:
     Angers and admirings
Heartsease and pity.
   No right without a wrong.

Since Eve put her hand out
   To start the primal fight,
     What's come of our enquirings?
The conduct of a doubt.
   No wrong without a right.

THE FIRST LESSON

Genesis 3, read as part of the broadcast Christmas Service of King's
College Chapel, Cambridge, 1975.

The choirboy's crystal voice retells the Tale
   Would mend and moral us, Church Fathers thought.
   The Tale would have us maim our founding ought
And what most dignifies Man's state assail.

Obedience, well by her withheld from Wrong,
   Declares our dauntless Eve the original Saint
   Whose fabled deed now clears us of attaint,
Now, at long last, (what sin-filled years too long!)

Their Saint, for those, her like, who dare aspire
   'Gainst Holy Writ and its corrupted soul,
   Against its grim reversal of our role—
To re-make Man, that helpless Deifier.

Why shrink, O Prince, from canonizing Eve,
Although that Tale its own self misconceive?

CONTRA-FACTUAL IMPLICATE
1776-1976

Had the embattled farmers fired no shot,
    That soldiery by the Bridge having all deserted,
Turned farmers too, what now might be our lot,
    First Threat to the Great Peace thus averted?

No Civil War; in its place a Wilberforce;
    No World Wars: One, Two, Three...(each such a success!)
No monolithic state; no Ulstering, of course;
    No Vietnam crime; maybe no Bangladesh.

Logicians call this 'nonsense', will not let
    You dream of turning any clock back so.
They may be right. But let us not forget
    That out of Concord, Mass., can come such woe.

OLD NOTE

These quivering lines that crawl
   Across this littering scrap,
      Too faint now to be read?

Their aim, their end, their All:
   To minify the gap
      Between the Seen and the Said.

Nothing will recall
   What it was, that hap,
      When these lines too lie dead.

HERE & THERE

One's mind is what one is, not that which can be pointed at with a finger.

Cicero, *Scipio's Dream*

Two ways in my woods? No;
No ways at all, since every spray
Hides what might once have been a trail;
No sign of how to go . . .
Whereto? Wherefrom? We don't much say
Hereto, Herefrom. Passing queer
Is our common use of our key word, *here*;
Nor does our light on it much avail.

There goes with *where*; both deal with place
Rime well and herd with words like *care*,
Beware, prepare . . . Contrarywise,
Here carries a time, has even a face,
A speaking mouth at least, a share
In an individuality,
Teems with echoes that endlessly
Our strings of minims syncretize.

Here and *thence* both come from *he*
Who can alone be truly here.
(Though then I have to call him *I*
As all I know is his life in me.)
Neighbouring things can at most be near.
She, they say, is from deictic *the*,
To be pointed at not truly be;
What fearsome fears conceived that lie
Though from the first the soul's a She?

Though all it says no mind can know,
'I'm here' 's an utterance always true,
Unique therein, though it can lend
Its offspring some security;
Herefrom comes all I find in you;
All good, all ill hencefrom subtend;
Here failing, all that is must go,
Since whatever we'd have be so
Upheld by here its heart must be.

118

BIRTHRIGHT

'First to watch and then to speed . . .'

Francis of Verulam

When will it come—the smooth blade in the back
Anywhere, where's no knowing? There and then,
We hope, the prized quietus called 'The End'
Or 'the Awakening'. How now? How now amend,
Attending still to what we have in hand?

There's not a cog, a spider's anchor thread,
Muscle or nerve cell waiting for its call—
Taught by its neighbours that the Vast, the ALL
Turns, hangs on it—when backed against that Wall,
Knows aught about what will come after When.

'When' said, let's have a health: 'The Attack!'
Wrecking or Rescue crew! Homicide squad?
Here to arrest? As we'll well understand,
Not caring more than need be where we're sped.

POSSESSION

Whose hands were these,
Familiar though unknown,
Laid suddenly on mine?
(Some long, fine, strong and clean,
The others, stronger maybe,
Grimy, furry.)

And with no, 'If you please',
But as though they knew
What they had to do
And had a right to seize.

What have you done with me,
And through and to,
Who supervene?
What have I that's my own?

NOTHING AT ALL

For Roman Jakobson

Nothing at all can I guess,
    For all I do,
Of what in me says, YES,
    Letting What's On go through
        Or else says, NO.

Within my inmost mind
    It runs the Show,
Leaving me resigned
    Nothing at all to know;
        Yet it writes this too:
    That Who-cares-What
    Which rules me so,
    Lets me or not.
        And is the You
        It's speaking to.

ARS POETICA

> . . . in thy book were all my members written, which day by day
> were fashioned: when as yet there were none of them.
>
> Psalm 139: 15-16

I.

Conceive your embryo at its earliest age,
  The germ just entered the awaiting egg.
    What were you then? And how has what ensued
      Guided you since in all that you have done?
Before your birth, seriatim, page by page,
  That had to hold for *this* to be the peg
    Then placed; all hung on prior aptitude
      Throughout the climb to what was then begun.

Once born, your new-won comforts gone, you had
  To learn; harder, more hazardous, and yet the same.
    Each step prepares or it precludes the next.
The harshest lesson, this, on good and bad,
  The founding rule of the whole fearsome game:
    'Unto him that hath shall be given...'* Take in that text.

*Mark, 4:25. For he that hath, to him shall be given; and he that
hath not, from him shall be taken away even that which he hath.

II.
So poems grow. The lonely waiting phrase
   (How oddly often returning at the end)
   Plays out her game with words, friend after friend,
Faithless and true, too true, phase after phase,
Abandons, is abandoned, till arrive at last
   Lines in themselves secure enough to choose,
   Spot, see at a glance what they can use,
Forget thenceforth for good the chances passed.

What guides this life to what it comes to be?
   What led it through so blind a whirl of being?
   What served throughout as substitute for seeing,
Settled each loop and twist decisively?
   As well ask how two cells become a poet.
   But bear in mind that men may someday know it.

III.
Our mother tongue, so far ahead of me,
    Displays her goods, hints at each bond and link,
    Provides the means, leaves it to us to think,
Proffers the possibles, balanced mutually,
To be used or not, as our designs elect,
    To be tried out, taken up or in or on,
    Scrapped or transformed past recognition.
Though she sustains, she's too wise to direct.

Ineffably regenerative, how does she know
    So much more than we can? How hold such store
    For our recovery, for what must come before
Our instauration, that future we will owe
      To what? To whom? To countless of our kind
      Who, tending meanings, grew Man's unknown Mind.

IV.

Maker, remaker in your heart, poor man,
  Designer and contriver, how not comprehend?
  Nothing can save you save your own amend.
Sole beings who can reconceive a plan,
For nobler ends find means, why cannot you
  Even now remake yourselves, rid your life
  Of your old grim inanities of strife
And through your new-won hindsight aim anew?

Cast back now far enough, take in what's been,
  Learn whence you've come. Who then will dare to guage
  What's possible or not, or at what stage
We may be on our way to what demesne?
  Alive to this, what poetry still must do
  Not a few poets—forgiving Homer—knew.